Getting Ready for your Miniature Dachshund Puppy

Tammy L. Laird

Introduction

Miniature Dachshunds are one of the most sought after breeds in the US. I believe it's due to the large variety of options you have with this breed's colors, patterns, and hair type. That and their charming attitudes and the playful ways they continuously entertain us make them irresistible. In this book I would like to introduce you to the differences of the miniature dachshund and help you choose the right combination of characteristics for you and your family.

Once you've chosen the right puppy then we need to talk about getting your puppy off to a good start with training.

Raising a new puppy is no small task. What you teach him in the early days will provide the basis of how your dog will act for the rest of his life with you. So I'll talk about some of the challenges that you will face with this breed and offer you some down to earth advice on problem solving.

About this book

I started writing this book for my new puppy owners from Dog Dynasty. Then I realized there are many other people who need help with their new miniature dachshund puppies. Dachshunds are not like other breeds. If you have owned one in the past you know how special and unique they are . If this is your first experience with a doxie you will very quickly learn that they are very smart and know how to get their way. If allowed they will rule the household. They are masters at challenging you while appearing cute and cuddly. However, once they figure out how to get what they want from you they will push even harder. You just have to decide to be patient, confident, and persistent in getting them to do as you wish. I'll teach you how to train them instead of allowing them to train you.

I want you to understand that every new experience will come with challenges, but with the right mindset you can find good problem solving techniques to build a strong bond with your new family member while remaining the "Top Dog".

About me:
When I was growing up my entire plan for my future was to become a Veterinarian and own a small practice in town and spend my days taking care of animals. Well as we all know not all of our dreams come true. Sometimes life happens. Lucky for me, I found ways to realize my dreams in spite of the poo poo life can sometimes deliver. I decided to work with animals on my own terms.

One of my first jobs was as a Kennel Assistant. I worked cleaning cages and in my spare time I was playing with the cats and dogs and taking classes to become a

Veterinary Assistant. It didn't take long to realize I needed more. So, After a few more years I finished my degree and took the State and National Exams to become a Licensed Veterinary Technician. I spent 12 humbling years working at the Humane Society of MO in their Veterinary Department. Where I truly felt I had made a difference... not for the animals exactly; I felt like we helped the people in the community that wouldn't have had the funds to take care of their family members if it weren't for the services we provided at that clinic. Of course we helped the animals too. I just wholeheartedly believe that every person regardless of income should be able to know the love of a cat and/or a dog in their lives. It's what makes life worth it... the reason to get up every day.

While I wasn't prepared to drop everything and apply to Veterinary School. I knew there had to be more that I could give. So, I went back to school and decided I would try my hand at teaching. I thought I had found my calling in life when I got the opportunity to design a Veterinary Technology Program from Scratch in St. Peters MO. I absolutely loved the time I spent teaching and getting to know the young men and women that, like me, wanted to spend their life helping animals. I literally got to spend my days talking about animals. What was missing is the time I lost not being around animals on a daily basis.

So, my husband, Steve, and I moved back to his hometown of Metropolis, Illinois. Where we started our farm. We decided to work from home and we ran a successful boarding facility for both dogs and cats. We tried our hand at grooming... and did pretty well. However, our favorite thing we spent time on was our breeding programs. That was it. We found "THE" Thing that we were meant to do.

Today, we spend most of our time with our grandchildren and our dogs. I get to use a little bit of everything I've learned over the years to help raise healthy happy Miniature Dachshunds. With the added bonus of being able to teach our new puppy owners everything they need to know about starting their new family. So maybe my dreams did come true!

A little about our breeding program.
We have several breeding pairs in our program and each breeding pair lives in a different Guardian Home. Our guardian homes are made up of our Adult Children(Yes, that is how I see them. LOL), Our Mothers, my best friend and another set at Steve's best friend's home. So as you can tell there are several dogs that are part of our pack. I make weekly visits to make sure everyone is happy, healthy, and getting environmental enrichment to ensure they are well adjusted in their own homes. When our females become pregnant they receive hands on prenatal care. Two weeks before delivery the momma's come

home with Steve and I and live in our home. We help them through delivery and make sure momma and babies are safe and secure. Momma stays with us until right before her babies go to their forever homes. Then momma goes back to her Guardian Family.

The first weeks of a puppy's lives are spent being introduced to new environments and people. We want to make sure our babies get the proper socialization and environmental stimuli to lessen the stress that they will experience when entering their new homes at 8 weeks old. Once our babies are placed in their new homes I encourage my new families to reach out to me with any challenges that might arise for them. I'm also always available to answer any questions you all might have about our program …

Find me at:
Tammy Lynn Laird
tammy@dogdynasty.com
www.dogdynasty.com
Facebook: Dog Dynasty Puppies
Instagram: Puppies at Dog Dynasty
Twitter: Dog Dynasty Puppies

Getting Ready for your Miniature Dachshund Puppy

If you've ever been owned by a Doxy before you know that they are big dogs in a little package. If you are planning on getting one just know they will win over your heart immediately. They have a way about them that makes us fall head over heels in love. Once you have one in your life you will never go back to a life without one, two, or five (trust me).

I'm not sure where to add this in the book, but once you have a doxy... You will never visit the bathroom alone again. You should prepare yourself for this. Oh and the "fact" that a dachshund demands to sleep with you. My husband absolutely refused to allow a dog to sleep in his bed...before we got a doxie. They demand it in the cutest way possible. I've yet to meet the person who can say NO to a doxy!

You will find in this book that I use many different names for Miniature Dachshunds while writing about them. That's because they have lots of different nicknames. Some of it depends on where you live. Others are just cute nicknames for them.

Nicknames for Dachshunds

Doxy, Doxie, Dochsie, Dash Hound, Weiner Dog,
Wiener Dog, Hot Dog, Sausage Dog, Dotson, Doxin,
Daschie, Long Dog to name a few.

Pronunciation

If you want to be proper, the name should be pronounced
with a German accent – DAKS-huunt (or hoont)

Origin of Dachshunds

It is widely accepted that the Germans were responsible
for the development of the dachshund hundreds of years
ago to hunt Badgers. Their short muscular legs keep
them low to the ground to track scents, and their narrow
bodies allow them to crawl into burrows, looking for
badgers. Despite their small size, Dachshunds are brave
and fierce.
The three varieties of dachshund, smooth-, wire-,and
long-coated, originated at different times. The smooth
was the first and came from a mixture of a miniature
French pointer and a pinscher.

Temperament

The dachshund is highly intelligent, sweet, loving, charmingly playful, courageous, and sometimes a very stubborn dog. They are affectionate and loving to their family and strive to be the center of attention. They are protective of their environment and family members and will bark when sensing a potential threat. If needed they will defend their family with their lives.

Hair type

Dachshunds have three very different coat types.
Shorthaired (smooth coat): this is the most common coat. It is smooth, short, and sleek.
Longhaired: the hair is fuller, fluffier, sometimes has curly or wispy ears, longer skirt, full chest, frilly legs, long tail with hair that drapes down from it known as a fan, they will grow hair between the toes that needs to be groomed every month or two. A coat of a longhair does not develop fully until the dog is a year and a half to three years old.
Wirehaired: very wiry coat with a harsh feel. However, there are different wirehaired subtypes. For the purpose of this book I will list them as rough, soft, and silky.

*From left to right: wire, long hair, smooth coat

Color(s) and Patterns

Dachshunds have a larger variation of colors, patterns, and coats than any other breed. I could write a whole book on the color combinations and their meanings. For this book I am going to do a quick overview to show you the vast amount of choices you have when looking for your soul mate.

Solid color-the whole dog is one color. Their colors include **Black, Chocolate, Red, Cream, Isabella(purplish tent), Blue(Gray), Extreme White, with dilutes, and non dilutes.**

*shades of Red

Solid Black is said to be the rarest dachshund color in the world. You may also come across a true Albino.

*pure black smooth coat puppy

Albino- Albinism is a fairly rare genetic mutation that causes a complete lack of pigmentation. They will have a uniformly white coat with pink paw pads, pink skin around their eyes, their eyes will not have pigmentation and they will very likely be blind.

This is very different from an **extreme white dachshund** that can be 75% - 100% white, along with non - pink color in their nose, paw pads, and eyes.

*extreme white long hair puppy

Shaded- This is a solid colored coat that has an overlay of black hair down the back, ears, and tail that causes a shading effect

*Shaded Red smooth coat puppy

Points- The points are the accent colors (or a secondary color) any base color can have points, but they always make me think of a Rottweiler's color
 Pattern.

*black with cream points

Tuxedo- Usually has a white chest, some white on collar, white feet, white tip of the tail.

Dapple- Spots or patches of dilute pigments against the base coat color. Even if there is only a small spot of dappling on the coat your dog will be considered a dapple.

Hidden Dapple- Meaning the dog is technically a dapple but the dappling is disguised or hidden. Most commonly found in Red colors, but is also seen in black and creams. You may also find a darkened pigmentation(spots) on the tongue or the roof of their mouth. The only true way to know is by knowing the parentage of that dog or doing a DNA test for color.

Double Dapple- This is when both parents are dapple(merle) they pass on two sets of the merle gene. These dogs tend to show large white areas on the body and will usually not have symmetrical markings. Double Dapple Dachshunds can be Deaf, Blind, or Impaired and have allergies. There are many more health concerns with this color pattern.

Piebald- will have one or two base coat colors along with approximately 50% of the body being covered with white.

*Red piebald with ticking smooth coat puppy

Brindle-will have a base coat with a different color striping along the body. Can be entire body or partial coverage. Actually, It will cover all of the body but may not show up visually on the entire body.

Wild boar- Only occurs in shorthaired and wirehaired dachshunds. This is a pattern where nearly all the guard hairs are producing three or sometimes four colors on each individual strand of hair while the undercoat is a solid color.

Sable- Is very similar to the wild boar, but seen in only long hair dachshunds.

Ticking-Small colored spots on white areas. It looks like someone splattered paint over their body.

Parti- Is three different colors along with white.

Brapple- A combination of brindle and dapple.

Harlequin- turns white all the dilute areas caused by dappling, making the dog not appear to be dappled.

*There are more variations of colors and patterns out there. This is just a quick overview of what you can look for in this breed.

Size

According to the American Kennel Club(AKC) and the Continental Kennel Club(CKC) there are two types of dachshunds. Standard Dachshunds and Miniature Dachshunds. Over the many years that I have been raising dachshunds I have found many variations. Even though we are here to talk about the miniature dachshund I think it is important to know what else is out there.

Here is a list of Dachshund Characteristics by body size.

Standard Dachshunds have a withers height between 8"- 9"
weight of 16 lb - 32 lbs as an adult
overall body length of roughly 21.5"- 25"

Miniature Dachshunds have a withers height of 5"- 6"
Weight of 11lbs or under as an adult
Average Body Length of 14"
Chest circumference of 14 - 15 inches

Tweenie Dachshund have a withers height of 6"- 7"
typically weigh between 11lb - 16lbs

*It's important to note that "Tweenie" is not an official term and is categorized as anything between the miniature and standard size

Kaninchen (German for "Rabbit") according to the World Canine Federation, any dachshund that weighs less than 3.5 kg (7.7 lbs) and has a chest measurement of 30 centimeters around (11.8 inches) or less is classified as a kaninchen.

I have one more opinion about this size chart. I believe a miniature dachshund can weigh slightly more than 11lbs and still be considered a Miniature. It is my opinion that some miniature dachshunds that are longer than 14 inches in length may weigh a bit more than the 11lb cut off and still be a "real" Miniature Dachshund.
I would also like to add that these weight requirements are for dogs that are the appropriate weight for their body size. Meaning they are not overweight or fat.

Life Expectancy: 12 - 16 years
I have seen miniature dachshunds live to 20 years and still be lively, vibrant, and healthy.

Where to find a Miniature Dachshund

When it comes to finding your new best friend, Dog Dynasty is your best option. We have been raising mini's for over 20 years. You can visit our website at www.dogdynasty.com. Find us on Facebook at Dog Dynasty Puppies where you can see tons of pictures and videos of our babies growing and playing. If you have any questions we encourage you to call or text us at 618-309-3733 so we can answer all of your questions directly.

(What? Did you not expect me to advertise myself in this book ;)

Reputable Breeders

I have found reputable breeders online through Facebook, Instagram, Twitter, all over social media. In today's world you have to stay relevant and easy to find. It is up to you, the consumer, to protect yourself from the hundreds of thousands of scammers that are out there waiting to take your money.

All kidding aside, there are plenty of good breeders out there. When I'm searching for new blood lines here are some places that I start at. AKC(American Kennel Club) and CKC(Continental Kennel Club) both have lists of Reputable Breeders along with advertisements of new litters that are available. I look on Facebook, Instagram, Twitter, Pinterest, and other social media sites to see who is advertising. I have also gone to Google Maps and put in Dachshund Breeders and the State that I am looking in. You will get a list and a location so you can check them out a little bit. In the past I have visited Craigslist, but I have to tell you. 95% of the animals on there have Red Flag written all over them. In addition to these places. Don't forget to check Dachshund Groups for hunting, field trials, or just dachshunds fun sites where you can meet like minded people and see where they got their doxies from.

Puppy Scammers:

It's important to be aware of and protect yourself from a Puppy Scammer(s). I have personally experienced hundreds of them over the years and the number seems to be increasing daily. They are people who pretend to be a reputable breeder, sometimes stealing that breeder's pictures and information, and using it to take advantage of people shopping for a new puppy online. They usually ask for you to send them money after showing you their adorable pictures. Once they receive your money they ghost or block you. You, in return, never receive your puppy or any follow up information. There is something you can do… Be a proactive consumer! Look for the Red Flags! Double check references! Personally, I encourage my new puppy owners to post on our Facebook Page (Dog Dynasty Puppies) and give us updates about their babies. This does two things. First, it helps me keep an eye on our puppies and how they are growing. Second, it gives potential new puppy owners a place where they can choose several different people to contact and get an honest review of our puppies and continued commitment to our new puppy owners.

Red Flags:

The price is too good to be true. You have been searching for a puppy for months and all the prices are pretty high. Well this person has great looking puppies… and they are at a great price.
*Reputable breeders that charge a high price for their puppies are not trying to get rich. It is quite expensive to raise well adjusted and emotionally sound puppies, provide their routine medical care, socialize those puppies to get them ready for their new homes, Provide individual care for each puppy to make sure they will be happy and healthy. There is lots that goes on to prepare new puppies to go to their new homes.

Sketchy Communication. When the breeder "ONLY" wants to communicate with you by email or text.

*Reputable breeders will talk to you by phone or video chat with the puppy in the video, or in person. They will also answer all of your questions.

*I personally communicate a lot by text with potential puppy clients. However, I am always available to take phone calls or meet in person.

Broken English. This is a little bit of a touchy subject. Let me start by saying not all people with broken English are scammers. It has just been reported that a large number of foreigners have been caught doing it. With that being said, I have lots of friends and puppy owners that use broken English.

Odd Payment Options. The person asks you to wire them the money(western union, moneygrams, etc.), pay by money order, transfer the money through Walmart, pay by gift card. Sometimes they will say this is fully refundable or if for any reason you want to transfer that amount to another puppy that is an option. Biggest Red Flag is to ask you to pay for the puppy in full upfront. These are all huge Red Flags.

*Reputable Breeders will require a small deposit to hold your puppy. This is usually a non-refundable, non-transferrable payment of one to a few hundred dollars. That amount is deducted from the total price of your puppy. This is done to discourage the new owner from backing out of an agreement to purchase an individual puppy. Which can harm the puppies chances of being adopted in the future. It's human nature to wonder what was wrong with a puppy that made the first owner back out. When in reality the other owner just didn't manage his finances properly.

*I highly recommend paying your deposit with a secured credit card(they are insurable)

Purebred Puppy without papers- This is generally advertised at a much lower price than a Registered Miniature Dachshund. To me this is a very good setup for a scam. You have to ask yourself...Why? Why go through the process of breeding if you are not going to do the most basic things such as register that litter. If you aren't going to register why not...Is either the mom or the dad not really a dachshund or are they only part dachshund? Maybe they bred a Standard Dachshund to a Miniature Dachshund and couldn't get them registered. If they didn't register the puppies... What else Didn't they do?

*Reputable Breeders take the time to dot all of their I's and cross all of their T's. Meaning they want to make sure they are breeding to better the breed. We make the best possible choices to ensure the perfect puppy is produced, grown to adulthood, and registered for the future. If you aren't registering your litters ... It's my opinion that you are just trying to line your pocket book. Not do what's best for your animals.

I have also had people call and ask me if I will sell them a puppy cheaper if they don't want the papers, because they are not looking to breed. I personally think once you adopt your puppy from us it is your choice to breed that animal or not, but I send them out into the world as full fledged Miniature Dachshunds.

The dog is free but you pay for shipping. This is rare, but I've seen it. Please do not fall for this.
*The red flag is the free part. Shipping a puppy is an actual option. I don't recommend it, but it is something that is done on a regular basis. I will, however, personally deliver your puppy to your door, for an additional fee.

Sad Story of why they need to rehome a purebred Miniature Dachshund. While this can happen. The person is either not being honest with you or is not being honest with the reputable breeder that they purchased the puppy from. All Reputable Breeders have a contract stating they will take their puppy back at any time during its life. For any reason.

Price increases after the deposit. This should be a huge red flag. When you place your deposit it is on a specific puppy at a specific price.

*Any one of these signs is not enough to decide a person is a scammer.
This list is just to get you to consider all of the information about a breeder
and make the best decision for you.

What can you do to make sure you are not being scammed

Meet with your breeder at their home- The best thing you can do is meet your breeder in person and see your new puppy to make sure they are a good match for you. If this is not an option because of distance, the next best thing is to spend some time speaking over the phone or video chatting. Ask to see your puppy during the video chat.

Ask questions-Reputable Breeders love to talk about their breed and educate new owners on how to properly care for their new babies. Ask about How big the parents are? What colors are the parents? If there are any medical issues or congenital defects that the breeder is aware of or tested for? What type of temperaments do mom and dad have? What vaccinations will the puppy have before going home and what vaccines will (s)he still be required to get once you take him home?

Get documentation-make sure before leaving with your puppy you have received their Registration Paperwork,

Vaccination Records, Microchip information, and a copy of the Adoption Contract for your records.

Getting your dachshund from a Humane Society, Rescue, or Shelter

I support Humane Societies, Rescues, and Shelters and I believe they provide a great service to the animals that have been abandoned. I've spent many years working at the Humane Society of Missouri. With that in mind, here are some things to consider when getting a puppy or adult dog from one of these places.

Most, but not all, dogs that have been abandoned to a facility have been put there because they had issues the last owner could not commit to finding a solution for. Or that owner caused the problems because they were irresponsible dog owners. This means that when you get this dog you will not only be starting at the beginning with behavioral training. You are actually needing to Re-train them. Meaning you must stop the dog from the bad behavior while also teaching the right one. This is a noble thing to do for someone who has the time, patience, and stamina to take on such a big task. I applaud those people and I have adopted many animals myself over the years. That is why DOG DYNASTY makes a concerted effort to stay in contact with its new families and if for any reason they can no longer take care of their baby, (s)he is always welcome back at our home no matter the reason. We have faithfully stood behind this statement and included it in our adoption contract for over 20 years.

Then there are the people that want to know what they are committing to. What is the exact date of birth of your new puppy or dog? What colors were his parents? What is this new puppy going to grow up to look like? Will he shed a lot or a little? Is he a barker? What size will he be? What distinctive traits will he have? How healthy were the parents? Are there any genetic abnormalities that you'll need to be aware of? And so many more questions that cannot be answered by a place that has not personally spent time handling and caring for the puppy every day of its life and has been there every day of its parent's and grandparent's lives.

Keep in mind that this statement is made with the knowledge that… if you've acquired my book you have already made up your mind to look for a new Miniature Dachshund Puppy.

Routine Care

You are responsible for the well being of a new Mini Dachshund. He will require proper nutrition, a stimulating and safe environment, yearly veterinary care starting with the first check up within 72 hours of coming home. You will need to establish a good routine for your puppy to follow from the beginning.

Grooming Requirements:

Dachshunds are generally very clean dogs with little to no body odor. Maintaining your mini dachshund should include clipping his nails, cleaning the inside of his ears(I use a soft tissue), and bathing when necessary. Wirehaired and longhaired dachshunds may require professional grooming and occasional brushing.

However, the only time I cut my dachshund's hair is … when clipping the hair between his toes. I do this once a month to every other month. I personally like my long haired doxies to keep their hair long. I believe if you cut it you're going to ruin it, but that's just my opinion. Another thing any dachshund owner (who has owned both a long hair and a short hair at the same time) will tell you. Short Haired doxies shed more than the longhaired. It's just a fact.

If you decide to seek out a professional groomer. Try not to choose one based on being the cheapest in the area. You want to take a little time and make sure you and your pet like the person. Ask if they have references. Stop in and observe how the groomer is interacting with the animals while (s)he is grooming them. Always remember that your dog is a great judge of character. So, if your dog doesn't like them, then you should check them off your list. I don't think it is acceptable to ask if you can stay and watch while your pet is being groomed. Your dog WILL NOT behave the same way with you there. They will keep looking at you to save them from the experience of being groomed. This will make it impossible for the groomer to develop a good relationship with your dog. My advice is if you are unsure of the person do not leave your dog with them. Period. Another reason to pass on a groomer is if they ask you to sedate your dog for services. A good groomer should be able to calm any dog down and get him used to being handled in a safe environment without drugs. If they insist on sedation. Look elsewhere. If your dog is a terrible patient then you need to learn how to groom him yourself. It is not fair to your dog or the groomer to force him into a stressful situation. It will end with someone getting hurt.

You might want to know why I'm so against a simple sedation. I believe it is an unnecessary risk to sedate a dog for something so trivial. If you do not work with a dog and slowly get him used to being handled appropriately you will always be sedating him. Then when they get older you are truly putting his life at risk. A good groomer will work with your dog and make every visit a positive experience. While working him through the grooming process a little more each visit. It can be an expensive experiment. But it's worth it to get the desired result. It is your job as the owner to not spoil your dog so bad that other people cannot touch him.

This is also a very good reason to get your puppy from a reputable breeder that introduces each puppy to many different positive experiences that prepares them for these life experiences.

*If you choose to bathe or groom your dogs at home. Please be very careful about getting water in their ears. I personally wash my dogs face, head, and ears with a moist rag. I never pour water over their heads. Doxies have long ears that will get moisture stuck down deep inside of them and cause a yeast or bacterial infection if not dried out properly. If I feel they need to have their heads thoroughly washed and rinsed with water. I take a fluffy cotton ball rub one side down in the vaseline jar. Then insert the cotton, vaseline side down, deep into the ear to form a seal. I then very quickly clean their head. Dry off their ears and promptly remove the cotton.

Never Ever put a Q-tip down the ear canal. You do not want to push any ear wax or debris down further into the ear. You also do not want to accidentally rupture the eardrum. This is uncommon, but can happen.

If you are finding an abundance of exudate(black or brown material) in your dog's ears. Or they are rubbing their ears a lot. Schedule them an appointment to see the Vet. DO NOT CLEAN THE EARS prior to the visit. You want to leave it alone and let the veterinarian see exactly what is going on.

Please do not bathe your dog more than once a month. Everytime you bathe them you're removing the skin's natural oils that are produced to protect their skin and coat. Bathing too frequently can actually cause a lot of skin problems in the future. If you don't appreciate your dog "au naturel" there are plenty of dog perfumes on the market that won't affect their skin and coat, but will make the time with them more pleasant.

** Please make sure you ask your breeder when they recommend you giving your new puppy his first bath. Make sure they haven't just microchipped your baby. If he was just microchipped you may want to wait about 48 hours to submerge him in water. Give the MC area(between the shoulder blades) time to heal.*

Fleas

I thought I would put this in around the grooming because most people think you can just bathe a dog and rid him of fleas. It's important for you to pay attention to this part.

How do my dogs get fleas?

Fleas are everywhere. Even if your dog isn't around an animal with fleas. You literally could pick up A Flea on your pant leg and bring it home. One flea plus a dog means thousands of fleas within one to eighteen days. Here's the important part... 5% of the fleas in an environment are on unprotected dogs at any given time. They jump on to get a blood meal(bite the dog to drink his blood) then jump off and lay hundreds - thousands of eggs in the environment. Yes, you read that right 5% on the dog meaning the other 95% are in the environment in different stages... Adult Flea, Eggs, Larvae, Pupae...Repeat.

Okay now let me start this by stating the absolute easiest way to control fleas is to prevent them and never get them to begin with.

DO NOT purchase OTC products. Please just go to the vets office and pick up the prescription brands. I know this is expensive to begin with, but much less expensive than the struggle with otc products! First the over the counter brands may have worked when they first come out, and in some cases they are still slightly effective. However, in the long run you are just throwing your money down the drain. If a product doesn't kill and prevent all the stages of the flea your pet and environment is still becoming a haven for fleas. Eventually they will over take your dog.

Now let me let you in on a big secret. The people marketing the flea products (even to your veterinarian) want you to believe that your pet needs to stay on flea prevention year round. That is not the truth. Most areas in the US experience four distinct seasons every year. If you use effective flea prevention through the spring, summer, early fall. You shouldn't have to use it mid-fall through winter.

When Is Flea Season?

Fleas tend to be more active during warmer months. They favor humid weather and temperatures from 60-75°F . Summer is one of the most active times for fleas and ticks.

The studies show that fall is one of the heaviest flea times of the year. That is correct… if you have not prevented the fleas and all of their life cycles…by fall you are fully infested with fleas! Once you have fleas in your home they can not only live all winter, but thrive all winter. However, If you use good products on your pet you will not see fleas in the fall and especially not in the winter. Any fleas outside will die during the winter freeze. Eggs can survive the winter.

*We treat our yard and around the outside of our home twice a year in the spring and at the end of fall. Making sure to use a pet friendly product, but still keeping our pets off of the grass and out of the yard until it is completely dry.

We use a prescription flea prevention on our pets in the spring and summer… saving the extra "fall and winter" doses for the following year.

*You may need to adjust when you use and don't use prescription flea products based on where you live and how the seasons change. Just know you can save some money on the colder times of the year…if you use good products during the warmer times.

Please note that preventing fleas is a different ballgame than having fleas and trying to then get your home and pet under control.

If your pet has fleas you absolutely need to go to your vet and ask for an adulticide flea killer for your pet and a safe adulticide for your home.

Just know that fleas lay their eggs all over your home in all the crevices and cracks of the floors, carpeting, rugs, curtains, sofa, chairs, teddy bears, your bedding, the pets bedding, in your closet, your dirty clothes hampers. You name it… they can get into it.

I have treated a home for a flea infestation many many years ago and let me tell you it's a nightmare. We 'Bombed" the house. Looking back, it would have been easier if that meant we blew up the house. No, we used bug bombs at that time and the family including our pets evacuated the house for 48 hours. If that wasn't hard

enough. When we came back in that was when the real work began. The dogs and cats were taken to the groomers to be cleaned and treated for fleas. My family and I divided up the work. I got out our vacuum and literally started vacuuming every piece of furniture and under them. Then all floors, carpets, hardwood, and oddly I vacuumed the drapes. I vacuumed until my arms felt like they were going to fall off. I then removed the bag from the vacuum and put it into a plastic bag, tied it and took it to the alley dumpster(that was back in the days when we lived in STL.) You don't want to leave the bag in the machine. Any flea eggs will just hatch and eventually crawl back out and continue laying eggs.
The rest of the family divided up by room and started removing all rugs, bedding, dog bedding, toys; those were all washed and thoroughly dried (It's the heat from the drier that kills the eggs).
We also had to mop through the house. Wash all the dishes to get the chemicals off of them. It was quite the ordeal.
Things I learned from this experience…

- Prevention is sooo much easier and cheaper than treating a flea problem.
- If you ever have a flea infestation… you have to retreat your entire home again every 7 days until you have killed all the fleas and every life stage. Which took a couple of months.

- Fleas can be in the environment anywhere. Just because you haven't seen fleas in your home or on your pets does not mean that they cannot pick up fleas from many different sources. People visiting, dogs or stray cats coming up to your yard, or onto your porch. They can bring fleas with them.

- You can unknowingly pick up a flea from your daily life and bring one flea home and end up with an infestation in a very short amount of time.

- Just because you haven't seen a flea doesn't mean they aren't there. They only jump on the dog long enough to eat(bite him) then they jump back off into the environment. The secret to finding out if your pet has fleas. Grab a cotton ball that you've wet down with water. Now rub it all over the back end of your dog around the tail and around their belly. Then look at the cotton ball. If you see a reddish-bronzy color. You are looking at "flea dirt" (flea poop). Nothing else causes that color on our animals.

- You can move into a home that has had fleas in the past and the eggs have laid dormant for years until they feel the vibration of you and your pets walking around. That vibration will stimulate the flea eggs to hatch and the fleas have an instant

meal. Then they start their life cycle all over again.
- Oh, when you treat for fleas you must treat every animal in the home. This includes cats. However, ONLY use medications specifically designed for your cat and one designed for the correct size of your cat. If you use the wrong thing on your cat no matter how safe the product is for the dog...it will kill your cat.
- Don't forget to treat your vehicles.

So let me state again that prevention is the safest, less expensive, less stressful option that you can choose.

Problem:

You bring home your miniature dachshund puppy (from a non reputable breeder) and you notice he has fleas.

Solution:

Before you do anything else. Go into your kitchen and make sure you have "BLUE" Dawn dishwashing liquid. Not any of the new stuff like the fancy sprays. You want the old blue stuff. Put your new puppy in the sink and wet him down then lather him up with the blue dawn. Scrub him really well and let that sit on your pet for about 5 minutes. Now rinse really well and you will see

the fleas and the flea dirt(digested blood) start to go down the drain. Depending on how bad the problem is you may need to do one more quick wash. Then dry him really well. Wipe out those ears.
Call your vet and go immediately and pick up a prescription flea preventative.

The Blue Dawn is a life saver. However, if you don't follow up with going directly to your vet. You may be setting yourself up for a flea problem. Fleas reproduce quickly...even if only one jumped off into the environment.

Crate Training

I crate train for two reasons. First, it's the easiest way to potty train. To quite literally train their little bladders to hold urine for longer and longer amounts of time.

It is said that you can expect a puppy to be able to hold his bladder for 1+ the amount of months he is old. So a 2 month old puppy should be able to hold his bladder for 3 hours. A 3 month old puppy should be able to hold his bladder for 4 hours. And so on. I will go over this more in the potty training section.

The second reason I crate train my dogs is to teach them that the kennel is their room. Dogs are den animals. While he is not going to like being locked in a crate away from his family. Once he realizes you are coming back to get him. He will start settling down.

I make sure our kennels are our dogs "Safe Zone" meaning when the grandkids come over our dogs have a place to get away from them if needed. Once our dogs climb into their crate they are not to be messed with until they decide to come back out.

How to use a kong to make crate training easier.

You should get two kongs one to use and one to be in the freezer ready to use. You fill them with yummy puppy acceptable treats - push the treat as far in the body of the kong that you can. The trick is to make it hard for your puppy to get the goodies out. Then when you have them loaded with treats you place them in the freezer so they will be ready to use when you have to leave your puppy alone in the kennel. The only time my puppies get his kong is when he is going into his kennel. I take the kong away when he comes out of the kennel. Then the puppy goes directly outside to go potty. The used Kong gets put into the sink to be cleaned... reloaded... refrozen... while the other kong is waiting and ready to be used again. Giving your puppy the treat when he has to be kenneled will completely make him focus on the excitement of the treat and not notice that he is being left alone. The trick is never allowing him to have the kong any other time. Your puppy will look forward to going to his kennel. Making kennel training one of the easiest parts of training a new puppy.

*No one else is allowed to go into our dogs kennels (No other pets and No grandchildren)
*Their kennel doors are always left open for them to choose to get in or not. Only closed when we decide they need to stay in longer.
*When you begin using the kennel **DO NOT** ever remove a dog from the kennel when he is barking or crying. You **ONLY** respond to your dog when he is calm. Or you will inadvertently train him to scream until you react! I will go over this more in the potty training section.
*If your pet refuses to calm down. Calmly sit down next to the kennel. Do not communicate with your puppy at all. Do not make eye contact. Just sit there and show him how to be calm, until he emulates your behavior. Then remove him once he responds accurately.

Before bringing your new puppy home

It's important to have a plan when you bring your new puppy home so that your first few weeks can be a smooth transition for both you and your puppy. So here are a few things that you may need.

- Puppy bed or soft blanket
- Collar and tiny harness and leash
- Poop Bags(for walks)
- Food and water bowls
- Puppy food… make sure you get the type your puppy is already eating. Or discuss safely transitioning to the food you prefer. Just make sure you change foods gradually so you don't cause upset tummy or diarrhea.
- Decide when feeding times will be. If you bring your puppy home at 8 weeks it is a good idea to feed 3 times a day. And be available to take outside directly to potty.
- Lots of small toys… we use cat toys for the first couple of months
- Puppy proofing supplies (Gates, Puppy Playpen, Crate, and some bitter apple spray)
- Pet-safe enzyme cleaner that's made to clean urine
- Paper towels to clean up potty mishaps
- 2 Kongs and Kong stuffing
- First Vet Check scheduled

- Puppy Classes Scheduled- I recommend waiting until he is all caught up on vaccinations before introducing him to other dogs or taking him out into the public areas.
- Puppy sitter-for future vacations
- Ramps or stairs for furniture to make it easier to get up and down from the sofa or bed
- A fenced in yard or designated potty area
- Most important thing- TIME
    - Time to get to know your baby
    - Time to play
    - Time to enjoy each other
    - Time to take him on walks
    - Teach how to walk on a leash and collar(harness)
    - Time to snuggle
    - Take to obedience classes
    - Teach new commands
    - To potty train

Things you don't have to have, but will want:

- Snuggle hound– heartbeat
- Puppy Outfits
- Coat
- Paw Protectors or shoes
- 2-way camera (for when you are at work)
- Seat Belt Tether
- Dog Car Seat
- Snuffle Mat

- Costumes for Halloween and Dress Up

*Extendable leashes or Retractable leashes are dangerous and cause thousands of pets to lose their lives every year

Extendable leash-Just NO! This was one of the leading reasons dogs were hit by car. Either off leash or the use of an extendable leash. These are dangerous.
Pinch Collar- not for use in this breed
Choke collar- it's just not a good idea with dachshunds. You don't want to be pulling on their necks. You are just asking for trouble with their spine.

Make a plan for:

Introducing your new puppy to his new family members (Cat or Dog)

Something you can try before bringing your new puppy home is to visit the new puppy and bring home something with his smell on it. Maybe the shirt you were wearing while holding your puppy can be put down for the dogs and cats to smell and start to get used to the puppies scent. So they're not so caught off guard when you bring the new baby home. They've already associated his scent within their environment.
Then when you bring your baby home you can start by introducing him slowly to the cat and dog. Let your cat do what it wants to do. If he wants to run off or get up high and observe the puppy. That is a good thing. Let the cat decide how and when he wants to interact.
With a dog you want to introduce them slowly to the new puppy. Making sure everyone is in a calm state. Most puppies are very happy to meet new people and animals. Your older dog may not be so happy to be face to face with a new annoying puppy. You should know that the introduction of new animals presents a problem for the previous pets. They need to establish their place in the pecking order all over again. This means your old dog may growl at the new puppy. That is okay. You should stand back and let them work it out. If you intervene you are causing the problem to escalate. The only time you should get involved is if your older dog

tries to bite or hurt the puppy. Then you need to figure out a new plan.

If you get your puppy from a different source then it is recommended to quarantine the new puppy somewhere in your home that can be separate from your other dogs and cats for 14 days.

Introducing your new puppy to your children:

I would set up rules that your children need to follow about the new addition. Discuss your rules before the puppy comes home. Make sure everyone is working together to keep themselves and the new puppy safe. Children under 10 years old should never be left unsupervised with a puppy. We don't want the child or the puppy getting hurt. We also don't want the two of them deciding to team up and get into trouble which is much more likely.

Things Children should never do:
- Children should never interrupt a puppy while eating
- They should never pull at their tails, ears, or legs
- Don't tease the new puppy
- Never take a bone or chew toy away from the puppy

Things we should teach our children to do:

44

- Teach them how to handle the new puppy with care
- Let them help with the feeding. It's very important for the puppy to see all the children in the house as being above them. When the puppy sees their food being given to them from each child it elevates that child's status in the pack. We don't want our children to be seen as their equal(littermate) who they would play rough with and continuously challenge to see what rank they hold in their pack.
- Let your kids help with the training. You can start with something simple like "Sit".
- Teach them how and when they can give a treat.

Things we should teach our puppies to do:
- In our house when the dogs and the grandkids get too excited and everyone needs to take a break… We say "Kennel Up". Ironically, not only do the dogs go to their kennels, but the grandkids go to their room. I always say we live in the dog house. Everything around here is dog related.
- Teach your puppies to listen to the commands of the kids. When the dogs go outside to potty when the grandkids are around I take them outside too. So they can hear the words or commands I use "Potty" and how I say it. The

kids are getting good at mimicking my tone of voice and behavior to get the same response from the dogs.

- Teach your puppy to never grab things out of the children's hands. Supervise your children or grandchildren when they have treats and make sure the puppy is waiting until the appropriate time to take the treat.

Make plans for how you will handle other daily tasks.

- Make sure that when you have to leave your puppy it's for a short amount of time … his bladder will need to be slowly trained to hold urine over time.

- You also want to confine your puppy to a small area (Crate or Playpen)when you are not available to watch him and care for his needs(potty time). This is what is most important to get him used to holding his bladder to urinate in the appropriate place (Outdoors). He should not be allowed full run of the house as he might chew on or get into things that might hurt him.
- Once you get your puppy home. You should limit the places they go until they are fully

vaccinated. That means they have completed their puppy vaccinations (usually around 4 months of age). It is very tempting to take your new best friend out to introduce to the world, but you are risking them being exposed to different viruses and/or parasites. The only place I encourage you to go with a new puppy is to the vets office and straight home. In addition to your vet finishing your pets puppy vaccination series they will also start your pet on a monthly intestinal worm preventative and flea preventative making it safer for them to explore the world with you.

- We all have times that we cannot follow the rules completely. You may need to run to the store to pick up a new collar or harness and have to bring your puppy to make sure it will fit properly. My suggestion is to hold your baby in your arms the entire time you are in the store. Never place him in the cart or on the floor where germs can be waiting for him. You will also experience people that find your baby adorable and just have to touch or pet him. I carry baby wipes with me to give to the person to clean their hands before touching my baby. I do not allow other pets to be nose to nose with my baby. That is a great way of picking up unwanted problems. In fact if I'm in public with my baby and he needs to have a potty break, I am very careful to clean his underbelly and paws as soon as I pick him back up.

*It's your job to protect them

Veterinarian:

Make sure you have a veterinarian selected so you can schedule your puppies first wellness check up and discuss his protocol for finishing his puppy vaccinations. You should have your puppy examined 1 - 3 days after bringing him home. This may require making the appointment before you bring your puppy home. Please ask your vet about their after hours emergency procedures… to make sure they have one. You never know when you may need this in the future. Even the healthiest pets can have an unplanned emergency. Knowing you are prepared may bring you peace of mind.

Suggestion: I think it's very important to hold your pet or keep him in a carrier while at the Veterinarian's office. There are too many things he can pick up from a Vet Clinic. Think about it… if your pet is sick, where is the first place you're taking him? They say parvo can live in the environment for up to 10 years. When is the last time a puppy was treated for parvo at that establishment? I fully understand the other side of that argument. If your puppy is current on vaccinations he should be protected from Parvo. Right? Not exactly! You see once your pet is vaccinated that vaccine stimulates the body's own immune response to the virus it was exposed to. Healthy non-stressed animals' immune system start to learn how to protect itself from that virus! So in the future if exposed to that virus again. His body knows how to fight it off. Well sometimes a fully vaccinated puppy will still get sick from Parvo… just not as bad. I've never seen a puppy die from Parvo that has been fully vaccinated against it. Long story short… As a Veterinary Technician that has been working in this field since the 90's I would not take that chance. Parvo is only one example of the contagious viruses that are seen in each clinic in this country. I still 100% believe in going to the Vet for vaccinations and health check ups. I just think you should use some caution.

*I am not suggesting any vet's office isn't doing everything in its power to protect its patients from disease(s). I'm just stating that you need to do your part to protect your baby as well.

- Emergency or after hours numbers- don't leave the first visit without one
- Flea and tick preventatives-Please invest in your dog's health
- Heartworm preventatives-Please invest in your dog's health
  - Please don't be one of the people that think... My dog will never be outside so he doesn't need to be protected from mosquitos that carry heartworm larvae.
    - It only takes one bite from a mosquito to transmit heartworm larvae to your dog. Mosquitos CAN get into your home. And be honest, even if you litterbox train your dog. He will go outside at some point. Just plan for the expense and buy it yearly(it will be cheaper in bulk). In miniature dachshunds you know your dog will stay at the smallest size for the medication. So there is a bright side-the smaller doses are cheaper.

- Secret that will probably get me into trouble with the veterinary professionals. A veterinarian will tell you that you have to get your dog tested for heartworms every year in order to get the next year's doses. That IS NOT on any of the literature from the manufacturers. Matter of fact it has been proven that a dog can take preventatives even if positive for heartworms. Not only is it safe for the animal that is taking the preventative. Because it only kills the microfilaria (babies) It is safer for all the dogs in that household and community. The dog will no longer be able to transmit heartworm larvae from mosquito bites to other dogs. By giving HWP you are essentially doing a slow kill of the Heartworms. Babies will die and Adults will live out their life cycle and die off naturally, slowly, and not cause the overload of dead worms that can clog the heart and lungs. So in short there is no reason that you cannot continue to get your HWP without the cost of the test every year.
- Vaccinations– Please note that you must keep your pets current on their vaccinations. Especially when they are babies. However, after

the first year of vaccinations. Meaning the year they come back after puppy vaccines are completed your pet should be able to get 3 year Rabies and 3 year distemper/parvo vaccination. It will cost more for these vaccines, but it will save you the cost of the yearly office visit and rabies tags fees. More importantly it's saving your dog from getting so many shots.

- Please do not let your vet talk you into scheduling your spay or neuter. Please fight for your baby's health. It is advised in this breed. To NOT spay or neuter until they are adults. That is 12 - 18 months old. I advise my new puppy owners to wait until their pet is at least a year and a half to two years old.

One of the biggest health concerns for this breed is **IVDD, or Intervertebral Disc Disease**.
What is it:
IVDD occurs when the shock-absorbing discs between your dog's vertebrae start to harden until they can't cushion your dog's spinal movements. They will go on to bulge (or hernitate) and compress the spine and damage your pup's nerve impulses causing paralysis or severe nerve damage.
Symptoms of IVDD(depends where on the spinal column the herniation occurs)

- Inability to stand

- Inability to walk or walk normally
- Shivering or crying
- Loss of feeling in (all or some) feet or legs
- The dog doesn't want to move
- Head held low
- Back arched

How to prevent it:

Important considerations to prevent this disease:

1. Purchase your puppy from a reputable breeder such as Dog Dynasty(www.dogdynasty.com).

2. Do not spay or neuter your miniature dachshund puppy until they are an adult. That means waiting until your baby is 12 - 18 months old. This will help both males and females to develop properly using their natural hormones. **(See section on Spay Neuter for further information)**

3. Do not allow your doxie to become overweight. (one of the biggest problems seen in this breed). As a society we tend to associate love with food and our little doxies couldn't be happier to share our meals. The problem is when a dachshund becomes overweight it puts an undue stress on their elongated backs and that is when a crisis can happen.

a. Don't feed table foods ... okay, this is a do as I say not as I do moment. Maybe, don't overfeed table foods is a better rule.
b. No(never feed) hotdogs they are way too fatty and filled with nitrates and chemical compounds used as preservatives.

Do:

- Do use pieces of their food as their treat
- Do cut the store bought treats into ½ or ⅓
- Important note: I do not recommend feeding treats until after your puppy is successfully potty trained. Every time a puppy eats he needs to potty approximately 10 minutes later. **(See Section on Potty Training)**

I've raised miniature dachshunds for over 20 years. I've shared my life, my home, and my bed with them. I've also read and researched every piece of literature I could find on this breed. What most of the specialists report in their books is that to protect a dachshund's back you must keep them from jumping on and off furniture and not allow them to run up stairs. Well, the specialists must not actually own dachshunds. I have stairs to all of my furniture so the dogs can get up and down… they do use them sometimes but there is no way to keep them from jumping on and off furniture unless you watch them continuously. And Keeping them off the stairs is laughable. I've blocked off our stairs. The dogs either climb or jump the fence. A determined dachshund is a force to be reckoned with. I tell you this because even though all the specialists recommend never allowing your dogs on stairs and furniture to save their backs. I'm here to tell you that life happens. Dogs are going to do what they want - when they want. And if you get a dog that is from a good reputable breeder, keep your dog on the lean side, and keep their nails trimmed (so they don't slip) their chances of hurting their backs is slim. Notice, that I didn't say there is NO CHANCE, just a slim one. There is a chance, but after all of these years I have not (knock on wood) had a dachshund with a back problem.

Spay/Neuter

Spaying and Neutering are considered major operations and require general anesthesia. With any anesthetic the risk of serious complications, including death, is always possible. Sex hormones are very important to the development of a growing puppy. Testosterone, estrogen, and progesterone affect the immune system, the musculoskeletal system, the cardiovascular system, as well as psychological development. Spaying a female dog is the human equivalent to women getting a complete hysterectomy. In women, removing the uterus, cervix, and the ovaries sends her body into instant menopause. It will do the same thing to a dog. Many veterinary professionals advocate for this procedure to be done as early as 4 - 6 months of age. The procedure was routinely done at the humane society to any animal that weighed over 2 lbs. In my younger days I believed this was in the best interest of the animal. You are brainwashed to think spaying a puppy before her first heat will prevent her from getting cervical cancer by 50%. And you're preventing so many unwanted pregnancies. You are not told all of the bad things that happen to their body because you've taken away those needed hormones. I have seen so many older dogs be abandoned at the shelter or put to sleep because the owners couldn't deal with the urinary incontinence that in many cases that owner unknowingly caused by having their puppies spayed at such an early age.

Pros(reasons to spay)

- Spaying can prevent uterine infections known as pyometra which can be life-threatening, although infections can still occur after spaying if all of the uterine tissue isn't completely removed.
- Spaying eliminates menstruation (spotting blood), attracting male dogs, and unwanted pregnancies. Dogs have a heat cycle every 6 - 9 months where they will menstruate for 1 week - 3 weeks. The time that she will be able to get pregnant is directly after she stops bleeding at which time she will be fertile for approximately the same amount of time that she bled. There are lots of products on the market to keep the dog from spotting blood in their environment or around your home. Most dogs keep themselves very clean and unless you are an observant owner you will not know she is bleeding.
  - **Solution:** simply walking your female on a leash to potty during the time that she could conceive will directly influence her ability to get pregnant.
  - If you're worried about blood getting on your furniture or carpets you can use washable or disposable doggie diapers and/or keep her in a room that the floor is easy to clean up (like the kitchen).

- Male dogs will mark their territory if left intact. Having a dog neutered does not guarantee they will not mark in your house.
    - **Solution:** If you notice your male dog is hiking his leg inside your home. Put a Belly Band on him and make him wear it while inside until he stops hiking. Once he realizes that despite all of his efforts... nothing is happening. He will get discouraged and stop this behavior.

Cons(reasons not to spay)
Spaying before 1 year of age:
- Increased chance of cruciate ligament tear (knee injury)
- Increased risk of back injury especially in Miniature Dachshunds. Their vertebrae and muscles do not develop properly leading to a whole list of back problems. The worst being IVDD
- Increased chance of obesity. This is not good for Miniature Dachshunds
- Increased risk of bone cancer
- Increased risk of hypothyroidism
- Increased risk of incontinence "spay incontinence"
- Increased risk of re-ocurring urinary tract infections

- Increased risk of urinary tract tumors

Neutering before 1 year of age:
- Increased risk of bone cancer
- Increased risk of hypothyroidism
- Increased risk of canine dementia
- Increased risk of obesity
- Increased risk of prostate cancer
- Increased risk of orthopedic disorders

I personally think the reasons to keep your dog intact (at least until after 12 - 18 months of age) far outweigh the reasons to spay or neuter. I don't know about you, but I want my dog to have the healthiest and happiest life possible. If I could do something to prolong my dog's life I would. I see this as a direct link to giving your dog a better life. If you are still determined to spay/neuter your miniature dachshund please wait until they are a fully grown adult… That is between the age of 12 - 18 months old. I would ask you to wait as long as possible.

Bring your new puppy home:

Register that Microchip

My absolute number one thing I recommend you do is register your puppy's microchip immediately. Make sure you give valid phone numbers along with emergency numbers. If you are anything like me the only time your pet is going to be away from you is if there is an unexpected emergency or a natural disaster. In which case you will not be available to rescue him. Make sure a very responsible family member's number is also added to your pets contact information. Someone's number that will not be changing anytime soon.

Deciding on a Name

I usually wait to name my puppies until after I have had time to play and watch them. To me their name should fit them. You will most likely be trying to come up with a name on your way home with your puppy.

Some of my Favorites:

Boys:

Vienna
Short Stack
Igor
Babushka Jagger
Sal or Ami (Salami)
Vader
Valerian
Cletis
Kielbasa
Wags
Luca
Earl
Jimmy Dean
Yang
Spicoli
Gandalf

Chew bacca
Hot Dog
Snoop Doggity
Smalls

Brat
Chorizo
Cool Now(TPB)
Denzel
Lanky
Wishbone
Picasso
Einstein
Oscar Meyer
Zander
Sir Barks a lot

Iggy
Toodle Lou
Frank
Goldilicks
Jupiter
Casanova
Kalypso
Vinnie
Loki
Dude
Link
Xavier
Rooster
Frodo
Morcilla
Zero

Girls:

Atari
Brooklyn
Bailey
Cora
Clover
Demi
Deva
Dakota
Freckles
Gabby
Half Pint
Indigo
Iggy
Jersey
Jinx

Half Pint
Indigo
Iggy
Jersey
Jinx
Kenner
London
Mika
Mocha
Oki
Piper
Phoebe
Pipsqueak
Quigly
Raven

Saffron
Sky
Twinkie
Tessa
Tori
Violet
Willa
Xandra
Zuri
Pretzel

Couples:

Betty and Veronica	Buzz and Woody
Amos and Andy	Fred and Ethel
Homer and Marge	Bart and Lisa
Scarlet and Rhett	Fred and Ginger
George and Gracie	Pongo and Perdita
Venus and Serena	Eva and Zsa Zsa
Kim and Kourtney	Linus and Lucy
Maverick and Goose	Thelma and Louis
Frodo and Sam	Pebbles and Bam Bam
Inky and the Brain	Twiggy and Squiggy
Yin and Yang	Ebony and Ivory
Fuzzy and Wuzzy	Hugs and Kisses
Calamity and Chaos	Parsley and Sage

Consider the fact that everyone with a smartphone has the ability to Google weiner dog names. So take this list with a grain of salt and use it as a starting point to help you come up with a name that is uniquely original to you and your family. For instance, my husband is a huge Star Wars nerd(I say this with the greatest amount of love and admiration). So we have had many Star Wars Character names for our animals along with names that we made up ourselves. (ex. when we bred rabbits– We named them TK421, TK422, TK423, etc.)

Food
Feeding your pet the correct food will ensure they have a healthy life along with a beautiful coat and healthy skin. Here are some things I consider when feeding a puppy.

What to feed

I encourage my new owners to stick with puppy food. Puppy foods have a higher amount of proteins and fat to support growth. This is highly important in a dachshund's development. I have several foods that I prefer for puppies. The one I send home with my babies is Diamond Naturals small breed. Most love this food and do really well on it. However, there are some puppies that don't like it or it doesn't like them. There have been some puppies that have developed flatulence (gas) from this food or upset tummy. That can happen with any food. The important thing is to find a good nutritional food that works for your family's budget along with your puppy's taste buds. You should continue to feed puppy food until your doxy is between 7 - 9 months of age.

How often to feed

8 weeks old miniature dachshund puppy should eat 3 times a day
12 week puppy and older should eat twice a day

How much to feed:

Many professionals will tell you to measure a puppies food to ensure they are getting the correct amount for their breed and size. I however feel differently about that. I believe puppies are like children and while you should never let them engorge themselves it is possible to let them decide how much food is right for them. When feeding my puppies I fill up their bowl and sit it on the floor at feeding time. I watch my puppy eat and when he is hungry he will eat without distraction. When he starts to look around at other things in the environment I remove the food. I compare this to feeding a baby a bottle. When they are hungry they will drink the bottle briskly. When they become satisfied they will slow to a lazy or leisurely pace. That is when they are done or close to done. I do this because not all puppies are the same. Some need extra calories at differing times of their development. When my puppy is finished with his meal. I pick up his food bowl and take him outside to the potty area. This is how he will learn to potty in the correct place.

Important tip- using plastic water and food bowls can cause an abundance of bacteria to build up causing doggy acne.

What type of food bowl should you use?

I highly recommend stainless steel food and water bowls. Matter of fact I would purchase 4 bowls. One set to use and a second set to wash. This is the best option for durability, ability to not build up bacteria quickly, and it doesn't leak

potentially dangerous chemicals into your pets food or water like some plastics, aluminum, and poorly glazed pottery. It's easy to clean and dishwasher safe.

Should dogs' food bowls be elevated?
In this breed it is recommended to elevate their food bowls. The elevation puts less strain on their neck, and if they're old or suffer from any physical conditions, it can reduce the pressure on joints and bones.

How often should you wash your dog's food bowl?

Many vets agree that you should wash your dog's bowl daily… If you feed with kibble, your dog's bowl should be washed daily, after the final meal of the day. If you feed with canned food or raw meat, your dog's bowl should be washed and sanitized after every meal.
I just throw my dogs bowls in the dishwasher, to be honest, about once a week. There are lots of things that the professionals recommend for a happy healthy dog. I believe we have to balance that with a happy healthy owner. Take all the information I'm giving you and decide what works best for you and your family and adjust it accordingly.

Potty Training

Our puppies (from dogdynasty.com) go to their new homes at 8 weeks of age. Between the ages of 8 - 16 weeks is when the professionals believe it is the best time to start and master potty training your puppy.

I believe the ideal age to begin housebreaking is when your puppy is 7 ½ to 8 ½ weeks old. You must begin teaching him where to eliminate before he establishes his own preferences. But don't worry if your puppy is older when you begin training, he will still learn through these same steps. It may just take a little longer. Your job is to be patient and consistent.

Let's start by choosing an appropriate place for him to eliminate outdoors. Most puppies prefer a small patch of grass. Try to find a spot that isn't littered with the activity of other people or animals. We want to find a spot that is safe and calm so he doesn't get startled or distracted while trying to do his business.

You will also need to establish a potty routine. Remember that it's all about being consistent. Start by carrying your puppy to the door and take his paw and make him scratch at the door. Some people use a bell that he scratches(rings). While others make a bark sound in hopes that their puppy will catch on. Whichever you choose, try to act out the behavior you want your puppy to eventually emulate every single time you take him to the door. Then you will lead him to his potty area(on a leash) and use his command word "Potty" to signal his elimination. Once established this will be the same actions every time he goes out to potty. No matter how many times you have to repeat the lesson.

If you take him to the same spot every time previous odors will stimulate him to urinate and/or defecate. Many puppies need 10 - 15 minutes of moving around and sniffing before they eliminate. Stay with your puppy the whole time. Potty training problems can result if you're unsure whether he has actually eliminated before you let him return to the house. And remember that your puppy needs to focus on the job at hand, so don't play with him until after he has finished up.

Once you have a potty spot picked out and you know your potty routine you should make a mental note of the times your puppy will need to go out. Here are a few examples. You should take him out immediately after he wakes up, after play sessions, 10 - 15 minutes after meals, any time he is smelling and walking around circling, before crating, and before bedtime.

The basic rule of thumb is to add 1hour+ an hour for each month he is old. So for a 2 month old baby…he will need to go out a minimum of every 3 hours. A 3 month old baby needs to go out a minimum of every 4 hours. A 4 month old baby needs to go out every 5 hours. And so on. If you brought your puppy home at 8 weeks and you have been working with him consistently he should be fully potty trained by 4 months - 6 months old. Most people that take our puppies home have told me that within a week they have their puppies completely potty trained. However, just like children, puppies have accidents occasionally. Maybe they are playing and they just don't want to stop to go outside and potty. If this occurs you just simply start over again from scratch and reinforce the original potty skills. Just the reinforcement will get them back on track.

Let's Get Started

Once you've established your routine it's time to get started. It's very important to be consistent with what you teach. By regularly taking the puppy outside, through the same door, making the same gesture that you want him to perform on his own, to the same site, and providing positive reinforcement (petting and praise) for proper elimination, he should soon learn to head for the door each time he has to go potty.

Sit him in the yard in the spot that you want him to potty. Always try to have him on a leash and use your command word "Potty". He will smell around and may start to walk away... gently redirect him back to the spot and repeat "Potty". If he relieves himself then give him lots of praise and lovins and tell him he is such a good boy.

If he does not potty…Pick him up without saying anything, take him to the kennel and leave him alone for about 8 - 10 minutes… Then repeat the exercise exactly. Carry him in and out of the house… so he doesn't have time to have an accident.

Remembering to repeat each and every step exactly the same way you did from the beginning. This continues until you get the desired result. This is the step that most humans get annoyed with and why our puppies don't get properly trained. Most people either give up completely or get frustrated with the puppy. Please remember … he is trying to learn (and make you happy) and you are his only teacher. So no matter how many times this has to be repeated. Your job is to remain calm and consistent. Remember the praise when he does what you want.

*Cat carriers are the perfect size for dachshund puppies

Crate Training is a must when potty training: Choose a crate that is the correct size... He should be able to stand up, sit down, turn around, and lay down comfortably. If the crate is too large... He will go to one side and potty and then lay on the opposite side. Each puppy should also have his own crate. Do not put two puppies in one crate.

Supervise the puppy indoors as well as outdoors. This will help you catch the puppy if he starts to eliminate indoors. You can also leash the puppy or place a bell on his collar to help you keep track of him at all times. When you leave home, put the puppy in a crate. When you cannot supervise your puppy, leave him in a small puppy proof area such as a crate. If the crate is large enough to accommodate the puppy as an adult, but a little big for him now, block it to avoid having him potty at one end and sleep at the other end.

*You may be able to use a laundry basket or pick up the crate divider from your local pet shop

Feeding: This is not play time. He should be directed to his bowl and you are to watch him eat, but not interact with him. If he starts to play. Just say NO, and redirect his attention. I feed my babies three times a day until 4 months old, then twice a day until 6 - 7 months old. It's very important to feed on a schedule so their potty habits can be maintained on a schedule. After eating they must go directly outside to potty.

Discipline: I NEVER EVER spank or punish my puppies. NO RUBBING HIS NOSE IN "IT". This just tends to scare and confuse him. Puppies want to please you … they want and crave your love and attention. If your puppy has an accident in the house… don't say anything to him. Simply pick up the feces in a paper towel or soak up the urine in a paper towel and take it outside to his potty area. Next take him out on the leash and let him smell it (urine/feces) and repeat the command word "Potty".

Please note…

- He probably won't potty at this time(he just relieved himself in the house), but he will start putting the smell, the place, and your friendly voice together… and figuring out how to potty in the appropriate area.
- Do not dispose of his urine or feces in your trash can in the house. That smell should be outside ONLY!

Important times to take him outside to potty:

- First thing in the morning without speaking, take your puppy out to potty (speaking to him may lead to submissive urination … aka an accident)
- As soon as he is finished eating… he should be taken outside to potty.
- After playing
- Any time you see him sniffing around … especially sniffing and circling
- After naps
- Before Bedtime
- At first it will feel like you are taking him out constantly. And that's okay… You're teaching him the routine. Before long your puppy will start letting you know he needs to go out.

Final Thoughts on Potty Training:

- Most people want to open the door and let the puppy go out and go potty on their own. This is great for older dogs that are trained, but puppies don't know what to do outside... They go out and run around the yard, roll in the grass, have a good time, then when they come back in... oh ya, he needs to go potty... so he finds a place indoors to relieve himself. So you should always go outside and make sure he is going potty in the correct spot and it is an absolute must that you praise him.

- Have you ever wondered why a dog(specifically a Dachshund) will not go outside and potty in the rain? How many humans have you seen take their dogs outside in the rain and stand there with them without making a huge production of it. Our puppies are learning from us. If it's a big deal to you... it's a big deal to them!

- Please don't use treats as a positive reinforcement for potty training! Puppies have to potty after every time they eat or drink. Physical praise works great!

- Water: Yes, you have to leave water down all the time. What does that mean for potty training? It means you have to watch your puppy extra close and take him out often.

- Remember the key to potty training your new best friend is being consistent.
- Potty pads encourage the puppy to go potty inside on rugs… in my opinion.
- What happens if your puppy potties inside the crate, in the middle of his training session? Take the paper towel(towel, blanket, etc.) whatever is holding the urine and/or feces to the outside potty area, lay it down,let your puppy smell it. Literally pat him on the head… bring him inside…then clean up the mess. His potty still ended up in the correct place. And we would rather build confidence than fear and disappointment. (You can bring the blanket back in when your puppy isn't watching. Just remember to clean it immediately. You don't want a urine soaked blanket laying in the laundry area. He may mistakenly think it's an appropriate place to potty)
- Your puppy will have days (rainy, cold, oops days) that he just has an accident. That is okay. You must not waver from the routine of cleaning up… put waste in the appropriate place.. And take the puppy to that area.
- In the winter months/rainy season I litter box train my puppy. Once I find a spot for my litter box that is where it will stay.
    - Comfortable, quiet place, with some privacy, no loud or odd noises. So do not

put it by the washing machine, hot water heater, or close to the kids play room.

- There are plenty of substrates for puppy litter boxes. My puppies respond well to the pine(wood chips) because that is what they have used before.
- If my puppy has an accident in the house while litter box training... I simply take the accident to the box and leave it... so he can smell it later and remember that is the appropriate place to relieve himself.
- If you decide to litter box train a mini dachshund. The best box I've used is the short but long plastic containers that you store things under the bed in.

- Some reasons your dog may not be defecating every time he eats. He may not be eating enough food at one time or often enough to push the stool through the body. Don't change food... just feed more.
- Slightly moistening the food with tap water may help to make it a bit more tasty.

Other Considerations when potty training:

Submissive Urination or Excited Urination is when a puppy urinates as a response to fear or anxiety. It is more commonly seen in young puppies who are not fully confident of their place in the world, but can also be seen in adult dogs. It is important to figure out what the cause of urination is so you can work to resolve the problem.

Submissive Urination is your puppy being scared of his surroundings. You should try not to scold him for this behavior; it will only make the problem worse. Instead, You want to find out what your dog is afraid of. Then remove that obstacle and start working on building his confidence. It could be as simple as he is afraid of your voice…maybe you've raised your voice or you're speaking in an angry tone. Maybe it's when he hears a loud or unknown sound. Or it could happen when someone new is walking towards him. These are only a few examples of what could be scaring your baby. Here is what he might look like when he is tinkling on the floor. He may try to make himself smaller, maybe curling up in a ball. Or he may be trying to get closer to the ground and tucking his head and tail. Another possibility is him rolling over and exposing his belly? These are clear posturing signs of a submissive dog.

Dogs that act this way are usually doing it because they are timid, shy, or anxious. In no way does this have anything to do with a dog being potty trained or not. So now that you know what to look for and a possible answer to why he's doing it. Let's work on solving the problem instead of making it worse by punishing him or in any way acknowledging his behavior in words or actions that will scare the dog more.

Guests should not come in and greet your dog... Instead they should avoid eye contact, do not approach the dog, wait patiently for the dog to approach them without him rolling over and showing his belly. Ask your guests to never bend at the waist and tower over your dog to pet him on his head or back. Instead they may kneel down and slowly pet the dog under the chin without staring him directly in the eyes. Or my favorite option...leave the dog alone until he gets used to having people in his home. You can start to make the experience a positive one by encouraging your guests to toss your dog a treat or two. This will take time and consistency before you will see a good result, but it does help to make the dog more comfortable.

If the loud or unknown sounds are causing a problem for your baby. You can work to slowly expose your dog to new experiences. Take a walk around town or the city. Bring treats and when you experience something like kids playing in the park. Take a few minutes... make your dog sit and then calmly give him a treat so he can start associating new sounds as a positive experience. If your dog is urinating because of your voice. Then you have to find a new way to express yourself so the dog isn't scared of you. Maybe the dog peed on the floor because you aren't walking him enough. In that case instead of yelling at your dog. You can take him on a few more outings a bit sooner and solve the problem completely.

If your dog is just anxious in general. It will help to spend time with him. Teach him a few new commands. Sit. Stay. Paw. Working with your dog and giving him positive reinforcement will help build his confidence which can lessen his anxiety.

We also have to discuss **Excited Urination**. I've experienced this behavior in overly excited dogs. They have an accident when they are greeted or when they are playing. This is a little different from submissive urination. Dogs will urinate or tinkle at an inappropriate time, but they will not exhibit the same submissive posturing. Instead he becomes very excited and urinates generally while wagging his tail and splashing urine around everywhere. If he is doing this while playing. Try to continue playing but calm down your voice and reactions while playing. The biggest thing that I have seen cause this is when someone is "baby talking" to their dog. This is when you use that high pitched voice and talk to them like they are a little toddler. As much as we love to act this way to our pets we have to ask ourselves if it's worth making the dog urinate on the floor. When you first greet your dog. You should try to restrain yourself from speaking to him at all. Simply walk to the door and let him out into the back yard. Walk out with him and allow him to run around for a few minutes to get rid of some of his pent up energy without a word from you. Then speak to your dog with a calm normal voice. He may still urinate a few times after starting this, but at least he is in the appropriate place to urinate. Don't pet him until he calms down. If you consistently do this he will begin to get better and stop the inappropriate urination altogether.

Urinary Incontinence:
This is usually seen in older females (7 years and up) that were spayed at an early age. But can happen in males and females of any age. This Is a medical condition that tends to happen while they sleep and may have a constant drip. Consult your veterinarian immediately. In many cases this can be resolved with medication.

Coprophagia (Poop Eating)
From a dog owner's point of view this is the grossest thing our pets can do. The Veterinary Technician in me knows that 9 times out of 10 it's harmless.

Most of the time this is just a behavior that the puppy has seen from mom. She licks their rear ends to stimulate them to defecate. Then cleans them up by eating their feces. Mom will also clean up their stool in the environment as the puppies get older to keep them safe from predators smelling the fresh feces. This is a very normal instinctual behavior that would have protected her puppies and the rest of the pack while in the wild. Puppies watch their mommas do this or smell the feces on her breath when she is licking and cleaning them essentially normalizing the behavior.

Like I said 9 times out of 10 it's a harmless behavior for your puppy. However, there is still a chance that it is a sign of something being wrong. Here are things to consider with poop eaters. Is the food that you're feeding a nutritionally balanced food? Are you feeding enough? Could your pet have parasites that may be sucking the nutrients out of the food and not allowing your puppy to absorb enough nutrients for himself? There are a few medical issues that can cause an increase in appetite such as diabetes, cushings, thyroid disease. Also some medications that can cause an increase in appetite. It's always a good idea to at least consult your veterinarian about these issues. It could be the first sign of a problem.

Here are a few ways to fix your puppies' poop eating behavior.

Consult your Veterinarian

Fixing any deficiencies with his food

The easiest fix is to go outside with your dog when they potty and immediately pick up the feces and dispose of it properly.

Adding a stool eating deterrent to all the dogs' food in the house. The idea of this is feeding the product to the dog changes the smell of the feces causing a bad tasting stool. You need to feed this to all the dogs in the house because if your pet is looking for a poop treat and his tastes bad. He'll just grab one or two of his friends.

Let's not forget that ALL puppies love to eat **cat poop**. I always called it their tootsie rolls(that's what it reminds me of). You must put your litter box in an area that your dog cannot get to. If they can get to the litter box they **will** eat the poop. I've never found a solution to dogs eating cat poop other than making it harder for the dog to physically get to it.

Diarrhea:

There are several causes of diarrhea in young puppies. Stress, which can occur at any time. Changing their food abruptly. Puppies are going to be curious and a bit mischievous so they might get into something they're not supposed to like the trash. Parasites are a common cause of diarrhea or your pet might have picked up an illness.

If your puppy is experiencing diarrhea the best thing you can do is take a picture of it and call your vet. That sounds a bit gross, but the first thing your vet is going to do is try to figure out how often your pet is having diarrhea, is it a mild case or is it severe. He will want a description of what it looks like(that's where the picture comes in handy). If you snap a picture and then try to scoop up some of the loose stool into a plastic bag. You can take the sample to the vet and have a stool sample examined to rule out intestinal parasites.

Or another problem may be that your puppy is getting sick. It's important to note when you notice your puppy isn't doing well. Assess his appearance...Is he being more sluggish than usual? Is he hypersalivating(slobbering/drooling)? Have you noticed a change in his appetite? Are his gums a nice pink color with a little bit of moisture on them? Or are they blue, white, dark red, brown, etc. Is he walking around with a hunched back like his belly is hurting? These are all things to take note of along with when you first noticed these signs appear.

If it's just a little bit of diarrhea or soft stool that is generally the same color as his regular stool chances are he will be fine to just keep an eye on and make sure it is getting better and not worse. Many puppies can get loose stool from simply overeating. I would not recommend giving any over the counter medications. Many are **not safe** for your pet.

However, if he is experiencing the signs listed above I think you should make an appointment with your veterinarian immediately to try to find out what the cause is and to make sure he doesn't become dehydrated. Vomiting and having diarrhea at the same time will cause dehydration very quickly.

General Questions to ask yourself:

Do you have a plan if your pet gets out of the house or yard?

It's a good idea to have tags on your pets collar. But collars can fall off or be chewed off. I highly recommend microchipping your pets in addition to tags. As much as I love microchips you have to do a few things to make sure your microchip works properly and gets your dog home to you...

First, is your pet microchipped? Have you had your pet scanned yearly at the vet's office to make sure the microchip hasn't migrated(moved to another area under the skin). Is your microchip information up to date? Do you have an emergency contact on your microchip registry? What I mean by this is if there is a fire, tornado, flood, etc. Something that will affect not only your pet, but yourself and family. Is there someone you trust who will be responsible for making sure your pet is safely picked up from his rescuer? If the only number on your microchip registry is yourself with your cell phone number and your home is burned down along with your phone. You won't be getting the all important call to pick up your pet. I always add my phone, my husbands, his mother's phone, along with one of our children's phone numbers. That way someone will be available to get the call and be able to respond.

Remember, A microchip is only as good as the information you link to it.

In addition to the above information, start your search for your pet immediately. Make sure you have current pictures of your dog. Make up a flier with all or your pets information. Identifying marks, name, even the color of his collar. Make sure you add your contact information. Take flyers to the police departments, animal control/rabies control in town, shelters, rescues, humane societies, veterinary offices, grooming establishments, pet stores, local grocery stores, any place that will let you post a flier. Then get on social media and make a lost dog post with the last place your dog was seen. Ask everyone to share your post everywhere they can think of. Look for specific sites on facebook that are for lost pets to post on. Post on local pages for the town's gossip. Just be vigilant about getting your pets information out there. You may need to repost daily. Just don't give up.

What do you do about your dog getting into inappropriate things like the trash?

If you are putting something in the trash that will harm your dog like chicken bones. The safest thing to do is to take the trash out to the receptacle. I don't take chances like this with my pets' health. However, things you can do to keep your dog out of the trash include putting a lid on the trash. If I'm having a difficult time getting my dog to leave things alone. I use an empty soda can that I wash out and put some pennies in. Then tape the top closed. I keep a close eye on my dog and right as he starts to get close to the thing I want to keep him away from… I shake the can and startle him a little bit. And Say NO! This takes a lot of repetitive sessions, just don't give up. It does eventually work.

What do you do if your dog starts Climbing over or digging under the fence?
Dachshunds in general are great diggers, they were bred to tunnel underground. My husband and I secure our yard with chicken wire around the bottom of the fencing and the rest of the wire is buried about an inch underground so when they dig to get out they are hitting that fence and cannot go any further. They will try it once or twice then they give up.
If you have a climber. It won't matter how tall your fence is. He'll learn to climb it. Dachshunds are very smart dogs. A friend of mine made a **Roll Bar** for the top of his fence that the dogs cannot climb over. I really don't understand it well enough to describe it in my book, but you can google DIY Roll Bars to keep dogs from climbing over the fence. There's even videos on how to set it up.

How do you keep your dog from chewing up your shoes? If you catch your dog chewing on your shoes. Promptly take them away and give him one of his toys to play with. DO NOT give him an old shoe to chew up and think that will work to make him not chew up other shoes. You just taught him that chewing up shoes is acceptable. My other bit of advice is to put up anything you don't want your dog to chew on. If you leave your shoes lying around out in the open you cannot expect your dog to just know better. When you have a puppy in your home you basically have a toddler. Try successfully reasoning with a toddler! It's pointless!

How about chewing up your underpants or socks?
I'm sorry to say this so abruptly, but this is 100% your
fault. Our used clothing will have an odor on them, even
if you cannot smell them… your dog can. They are
attracted to the mal odor and want to either roll in it or
chew it up. Your job is to pick up your clothing and
keep it in a hamper or area that your pet cannot get to. If
your dog chews up your clothing don't be mad and yell
at your dog. Just remind yourself to be better tomorrow.
DO NOT give your dog the item to continue to chew on
after you've caught him in the act. This is just telling
your dog that you think his behavior is okay and he
should seek out more items to destroy. Simply pick up
your chewed up item and dispose of it. No need to even
yell at your dog.

Barking at the mailman? A normal dog will bark at
someone coming close to your home. It's their job to let
you know someone is coming. So a dog sees the mail
man and barks at him, The mailman walks away. In the
dog's mind he got the appropriate reaction(mailman leaves)
to his action(barked and scared him away). Then it happens
again several times a week. To make matters worse
when you are home. The dog barks, you yell(Dog Hears
you "BARK") the mailman leaves. YaY! He did his job
again. Only you helped this time.
If you are going to be home when your mail is being
delivered. Talk with your mail carrier and ask them if

they would like to give your puppy a small treat (that you will provide) when delivering your mail so it may begin to be a positive experience for both your mailman and your dog. Your dog will start looking forward to the mailman coming by.

How do you make my dog stop Nipping at your fingers? This is one of those things that we start allowing because they are so little and they're not really hurting us. So why not let them play. If you want to keep your dog from nipping at you when he is an adult dog. Do not allow your puppy to softly nibble on any areas of your arms, hands, or fingers ever. It may seem innocent, but your puppy is learning how to interact with you from the beginning.

Allowing this behavior at any level lets your dog know that you're okay with being played with in this way. You are putting yourself on the same level as his littermates. And causing the problem to become bigger in the future. Please consider that at some point your pet will either encounter small children or older adults. By allowing this behavior you are setting your dog up for failure with children who have soft tender fingers and older people that their skin tears easily. Your dog does not mean to hurt you or your extended family, but if not taught proper behavior will become a nuisance in the future.

Your dog keeps jumping up on you?
You yell at him… "Sam, NO! DOWN!"
He just does it again. What can you do to make him
behave?
First stop saying his name to reprimand him! Name =
Positive Reward
Second, a dog cannot handle being ignored. When they
are doing something you don't want…turn your body to
the side. Look up into the air(think snobby girl pose– Nose
Up). If your dog runs around and jumps up in front again.
You turn again.
Do Not respond to your dog until they are calm all four
feet on the ground! Then look at him and you can use
his name and tell him he is a good boy. If this stimulates
him to jump up again. React the same way. Turn. Head
Up. No Eye Contact. Let him know and fully
understand that he will not get a response from you until
he does what you want.
*When you yell at your dog and say his name. That is a REWARD
for your dog. Any reaction is still seen as a positive reaction from a
dog.

Can you walk your dog off lead around town?
No matter how well behaved your dog is. No matter
how well he listens to you every minute of every day.
Please know that when a dog catches a glimpse of a
squirrel or other small animal across a busy street. HE
WILL CHASE AFTER IT.

Working in the Veterinary field for so long… I have witnessed sooo many dogs that were brought into the clinic for an emergency HBC (Hit By Car). They cannot help it. It's literally bred into them to go after small animals. It's as natural to them as breathing.
SO, PLEASE ALWAYS KEEP YOUR DOG ON A LEASH AROUND A BUSY ROAD!

Should you take your new doxie hiking or camping?
Yes, they absolutely love going on outings with you, getting exercise, and experiencing the outdoors.
I personally, don't allow my dog off lead (and secure harness) when we are out. I'm a little paranoid of him catching a scent (of a wild animal) and his hunting drive

kicking into overdrive. It is 100% natural for them to want to hunt. His hunting drive will over power his need to listen to you when calling his name. It wouldn't take long for your pet to get turned around in the woods and not know how to get back.

What if your dog gets lost in the woods?
It's different finding a dog in the woods than trying to find them around the city. There are a few things you can do to make the search more successful.

- Start the search immediately! The sooner you start looking the better your chances of finding your pet
- Put an item of clothing(that has a good strong scent) that smells like you or some bedding of your dogs. It just needs to be a recognizable scent. Put that in the area that he got lost or ran off from. It needs to be a place that you can check back often. You may want to put the scented item into a safe live animal trap to lure your dog in and keep him there. Ask animal control or local animal professionals for help with this.

- Place Lost Dog Signs or flyers in the campground kiosks, trail heads, anywhere people might see them, with park rangers, or other officials in the area. Post on social media and ask everyone that sees your post to please share it. Chances are the place you are camping has a facebook page where you can make a missing dog post. Most towns have a missing dog page on facebook. Try looking up each town in the area and posting in all of them. You might find hiking sites to connect with other hikers in the area. Put your thinking cap on and try to come up with any possible connection to the area through social media. We're all connected one way or another. And most people really want to make sure your pet finds his way home.

Make sure you list:

- A picture of your dog
- Description of your dog including any odd or identifying marks
- Last place your dog was seen
- Your regular contact information
- Your camping site information
- You vehicle description and plate number
- Maybe you know a person in the area that you can list as a secondary person to contact

- Make sure to contact the police departments, rangers stations, rabies control, animal rescues, humane societies, other shelters, veterinarians, and grooming facilities in all surrounding towns. Make sure all of these establishments have all the same information along with contact information as listed above. Someone might find your pet and if he's hurt take him into the vet. If he's safe but dirty they may take him to a local groomer to clean him up. You want everyone to help in the search for your baby.

- Try to get more people to help you search. Ask people in and around your campsite. Ask people you pass on the trails while searching.

- Along with calling out to your dog you should try to make sounds with his toys. Maybe you brought his favorite squeezy toy with you. It's worth a shot to at least try.

How to prevent your dog from getting lost in the woods

I want to take my dogs with me everywhere I go. I don't want them to miss out on our camping or hiking trips. I just make sure to keep a close eye on my dog while he's with me and in case of any emergencies his tags and microchip information are all up to date and working properly.

- Make sure your pet has a securely fitted harness that he cannot wiggle out of.
- Make sure he is attached to a lead the entire time you are on an outing.
- Make sure your dog has tags on his collar
- Make sure your dog is microchipped

What do you do if your dog gets sprayed by a skunk?
DO NOT GET HIM WET. Water seals the skunk oil secretion into the hair follicle and your pet will smell of skunk for weeks or even months. Instead, make a paste of blue dawn dish soap and baking soda then apply the mixture liberally onto your dog dry and massage it into the coat well. Then let it sit for about 30 minutes. Then it is okay to rinse it off. After you rinse off the paste you

will need to wash your pet with more dawn dish soap and rinse well. If you still smell skunk after this you can spritz your dog down with odoban spray. Just be careful not to get it into their eyes.

*The one place I always forgot to put the dish soap and baking soda paste is in their mouth. Chances are they got sprayed in the face with their mouth open. When you keep smelling the skunk's scent, but cannot figure out what area you've missed… guarantee that's it!

Why does your dog eat grass?

Animal professionals have tried to figure this out for years. There are a lot of ideas floating around. It's instinctual, dogs and wolves in the wild eat anything edible and have foraged for centuries. They may think it tastes good. Some suggest dogs eat grass because they have an upset tummy and they know it will make them throw up. All of these theories may be true.

The thing that you have to take into consideration is if your dog seems to be eating grass and vomiting often you may need to discuss this with a veterinarian. There could be something causing him to have an upset tummy that needs to be addressed to keep your pet from becoming dehydrated. If he's not vomiting after eating grass it really doesn't hurt anything. Just make sure there are no chemicals on the grass your dog is eating.

Should you be worried about your dog eating your houseplants?

Many house plants can be harmful or toxic to our pets. It is a really good idea to identify the plants you have and then look them up individually to see if they are harmful or toxic to your animals. If they are, please remove them from your house and yard.

I would list the toxic plants for you, but there are just too many of them and I don't know what most of them are. I just want you to be aware of the potential dangers of house plants and any greenery around your home.

What are harmful or poisonous foods that you should keep away from your dog?

Just because your dog likes the taste of something doesn't mean it is always good for him. It is your job to protect him from these types of harmful foods.

Grapes and Raisins- may cause severe liver damage and kidney failure

Avocados - contain a substance called Persin which is in its leaves, fruit, and seed. This can cause severe vomiting and diarrhea in dogs.

Corn on the Cob - this is not toxic to dogs, but it is a favorite of dogs to eat and become an intestinal blockage that has to be removed surgically. This is very common in the clinic around BBQ time.

Macadamia Nuts - contains a toxin that can affect your dog's muscles and nervous system. This may cause muscle shakes, vomiting, high temperatures, and weakness in their back legs.

Chocolate - contains a stimulant called theobromine. The most dangerous types are Dark Chocolates and Unsweetened Baking Chocolate. It can cause vomiting, diarrhea, heart problems, tremors, seizures, and death.

Fat Trimmings - Fat trimmed from meat both cooked and uncooked can cause pancreatitis in dogs. With Hot Dogs being the leading cause of Pancreatitis in dogs.

Onions, Garlic, and Chives - The onion family is toxic to dogs and can cause gastrointestinal irritation and Red Blood Cell damage. Signs are not always immediate and can occur up to a few days later.

Coffee, Tea, and Other Caffeine - can be fatal to your dog. Be cautious of your dog getting into not only the drink but the beans and discarded grounds.
Energy Drinks are a no no for your pets as well.

Milk and Milk based Products - can cause diarrhea and other digestive problems. It can also trigger food allergies which can cause your dog to be itchy.

Yeast Dough - needs to rise and will continue to do that in your dog's stomach. This will lead to the stomach and abdomen stretching and causing a lot of pain for the dog.

Other Dangers:

Artificial Sweetener - specifically **XYLITOL** also marketed as **Birch sugar** is fatal to dogs. It can be found in Gun Candies, Icecream, Peanut Butters, and many other foods and drinks. Dogs can experience a drop in blood sugar leading to loss of coordination and seizures.

Alcohol - not only causes intoxication, but it can lead to sickness, diarrhea, and possible central nervous system damage.

Cooked Bones- can splinter and cause possible constipation. Or worse it can cause a perforation in the mouth, throat, stomach, or gut and become fatal.

Tobacco - Cigarettes, nicotine patches, and other things with nicotine are seriously harmful to pets. They can cause severe vomiting, fast heart rate, drop in blood pressure, and seizures leading to death.

Cigarette Butts - Can swell in the dogs stomach or intestinal tract causing pain and intestinal blockages. Please make sure the smokers you allow around your homes clean up after themselves.

Bug Spray - Mosquito repellents contain DEET. In dogs it can cause tremors, seizures, and be life threatening

Sunscreen - If your dog licks sunscreen it can cause upset stomach, vomiting, and diarrhea.

ANTIFREEZE - even a small amount can be life threatening. Take your dog immediately to your Vets office if your pet gets into antifreeze. You DO NOT have time to make the phone call first.

Insecticides and Pesticides - can be dangerous for your pets. Please read and follow directions exactly.

Rock Salt - If they ingest this by licking it off of their paws, legs, or underbelly it can cause vomiting, spasms, and kidney damage. Please clean their paws, legs, and underbelly after walking anywhere you think they could have come in contact with Rock Salt

Rat Poison - I know you think this is a no brainer, but not only will you want to make sure your pets cannot get into rat poison. You really need to make sure you do not have it on your property at all. Dachshunds are very good hunting dogs. If they see a mouse chances are they will catch it and possibly eat it. If that mouse has gotten into rat poison … then your dog is going to also be poisoned from ingesting him. So make sure you only use humane traps for rodents. This may save your dog's life someday.

One thing that drives me insane is when I try to tell people to not feed these items to their dogs and they say… It won't hurt my dog. They've eaten it before and been just fine. Well maybe they didn't eat enough to get violently sick from it the first time. That is a blessing not a sign to do the same dumb thing again. Please understand these items have the potential to hurt or kill your dog. Please use caution and protect the health of your dog who depends on you to take care of him.

Here are some things that are healthy for your dog to consume:

Lean Meats
Fish
Apples

Oranges
Bananas
Seedless Watermelon
Carrots
Green beans
Cucumber slices
Zucchini
Cooked white rice and pasta
Kale
Pumpkin
Sweet Potatoes
Yogurt "PLAIN"
Blueberries
Cranberries
Broccoli
Green Peas
Tomatoes
Papaya
Leafy Greens
Oats
Coconut Oil
Wheat Germ
Wheat Grass
Apple Cider Vinegar
Coconut
Honey
Popcorn
Corn- NOT Corn on the Cob
Oatmeal
Bread
Peanut Butter- make sure it doesn't contain xylitol

To be honest, I've been a big proponent of feeding my dog ONLY his dry kibble for years. I thought changing their diet would cause intestinal upset and could cause other health problems. The only time I've fed my dogs table scraps was when we rescued a Great Dane from the Humane Society that wasn't supposed to live more than 6 months. So we decided to feed him anything he wanted. Steve took him to McDonalds every day and got him a cheese burger. He ate whatever we ate and as much as he wanted. That 6 months turned into 9 more years. He lived to be 13 years old. Which is incredibly old for a Great Dane. Their life expectancy is only 8 years. He was unbelievably healthy and vibrant until the day he passed away. I think that was when I started rethinking my stance on "NO Table Scraps". I do think dogs need a good base food that gives them the nutrients they need. However, I think as long as we don't give our dogs the foods that will hurt them(listed in this book) it's okay to give some table foods in addition to their well balanced dry foods.

I hope this book has answered some or all of your questions about Miniature Dachshund Puppies. I also hope that it helps you understand that there is lots of information out there about dogs. Please do your best to research the things that are important to you and do what you think is best for your pet.

www.dogdynasty.com

Dog Dynasty

It's a Dog's World

Made in the USA
Monee, IL
14 November 2024

70146557R00059